PATTERN

*The Restorative Power
of God's Embedded Word*

VICTOR R. BOYD, II

ISBN: 978-1-7341114-0-8 (Paperback)
978-1-7341114-1-5 (eBook)

Copyright © 2020 by Victor R. Boyd, II

All rights reserved. No part of this book may be used or reproduced in any manner whatsoever without prior written consent of the author, except as provided by the United States of America copyright law.

All definitions and scripture references came from:
King James (KJ)
God's Word (GW)
Amplified (AMP)
Easy Read Version (ERV)
Webster's Dictionary & Greek/Hebrew Lexicons

AUTHOR'S NOTE

The writing of this book was completed several years ago. What I've discovered since is that truth continues to expand; more than I would have dared to speculate. Finding the pattern not only embedded throughout more areas of scripture, but I've sensed what I can only describe as a harkening for it's authentic application. And I would challenge you to stay open

Husband to one,
Father to three,
Pastor & Coach
to the willing.

for what the Holy Spirit is doing in your life. We are not made to be cookie cutter people nor does God desire for us to hide in a corner with our bibles allowing life to pass us by. Bold adventure ready children of God are what will become of those who wield this revelation. And when trials, tribulations and storms come; we will find ourselves addressing them just as Jesus did when he arose and rebuked the wind:

Peace (Father) be (Son) still (Holy Ghost). Only after Jesus spoke these words in this order did the wind stop and a great calm was. (Mark 4:39)

PATTERN

You can follow me on Twitter: @Victor_Boyd

INTRODUCTION

Although some time ago, as a player and a coach, I remember we had points during practice that were called recognition periods. (Recognition- identification of a thing or person from previous encounters or knowledge) During these earmarked periods of practice we would key in on known tendencies that our coming opponent had demonstrated in the past. It was also a time to pinpoint certain tendencies we may have that need to be improved upon or adjusted. Recognition could vary from the type of play the other team would execute on a 3rd down during the 2nd quarter to how slow or fast the left tackle moves during individual running plays. So vital it was to take advantage of recognition time. Especially as a coach I noticed that it didn't stop at practice. I was always in that mindset. Recognize…Recognize… Recognize… It became a tool of life; seeing what had happened and adjusting for the next moment. For some time, it'd seemed that this was the best weapon ever, for all scenarios.

Bringing this recognition weapon with me as I left the athletic arena to pursue a life of ministry was a no brainer. I had already accepted that I would make some mistakes, well a lot of them. Just as I had in my previous career, in time I would recognize the pitfalls and begin to avoid the losses. Full proof, right? I even ministered messages with this "flawless" approach to victory. Stating things like, "once you know what the devil is going to tempt you with, then you step out of the way" (condensed version). Or try different prayers until you recognize what works, and then, you got it! Man, whatever! LOL.

What brought me to the clear end of this line of thinking was when I started to see how my losses so grossly outweighed my wins. Also, seeing how those around me were struggling to catch the onslaught of challenges and overcome them time and time again. What do I do? An answer was needed. I enjoy having clear cut answers. It's efficient and such a time saver. So, I took a step back from myself and turned to the scripture as I had done many times before. However, this time was different. For the first time my approach was not to read God's word through my personal experiences. I could see now that referencing my past first was causing me to relive them over and over. And fooling me into thinking I had figured something out. I was stuck on the recognition loop. This time I read the word and listened to what it was saying minus "me." (John 3:30)

The first place I ended up was in James 1:5-6 *If any of you lack wisdom let him ask of God, that giveth to all men liberally, and unbraideth not; and it shall be given him. But let him ask in faith...*

Now with a clear approach presented to me, I accepted that for victory to be consistent in my life, I was going to need God's wisdom. Not my wisdom with a layer of scriptural icing.

Now what happened next was interesting. I prayed, asking God for wisdom. Without a doubt in my mind that he would answer my prayer. Wouldn't you know it! He did! But he did it in such a way that if I really didn't believe he would give me wisdom, I would have completely missed it.

So, my goal in writing this book is to lay out the path that I was led to discover the victorious wisdom that I prayed for. Which he revealed to me through "The Pattern." 2 Timothy 2:15 *Study to show thyself approved unto God, a workman that needeth not to be ashamed, rightly dividing the word of truth.*

1

JOURNEY FOR THE BASICS

JOHN 1:1-2: *In the beginning was the Word, and the Word was with God, and the Word was God. The same was in the beginning with God.*

Never really knowing why John 1:1 has always stood out to me and still being a great lead off scripture when in a pinch. Suddenly became the focus of my treasure hunt. Reading the verse, kept bringing the question up, which I would become very familiar with through this journey; "What do you see?" At first all I could see was the same thing that I saw the hundreds of times I read the verse before. But knowing something unmined was here I continued to read and meditate, meditate and read. Then suddenly there it was. A pattern emerged from the repetition. The eureka moment was only dwarfed by my duh moment. The pattern is this: **START—PRESENT—END—START**.

Can you see it? The verse states that the Word was in the beginning (**START**), then the Word was with God (**PRESENT**) because it's Him (**END**). Now verse 2 Recycles the Word back to the beginning (**START**). That's it; "**THE PATTERN!**" Oh yeah! Okay, great, but now what? Much like any renovation project, things get ugly before they get better. Not truly sure what this **START—PRESENT—END—START** thing means, I decided to keep my pursuit simple. This means that I've already concluded that I know nothing. And God has given me this much so; I'm just going to trust the Holy Ghost to continue to guide me. John 16:13 (GW) *When the Spirit of Truth comes, he will guide you into the full truth.*

2

START—PRESENT—END—START

Let me first state that all of this hide and seek didn't take place all at once. As I trusted in the Lord vowing not to look at his word through my own eyes but instead to let his light reveal itself purely. Psalm 32:8 (AMP) *I will instruct you and teach you in the way you should go; I will counsel you [who are willing to learn] with My eye upon you.*

I found myself reading Proverbs as I try to do daily as a discipline. In reading Chapter 4, there were some keywords used here that struck me. To the point, **WISDOM**, **INSTRUCTION** and **UNDERSTANDING**. First, let's unwind the words:

WISDOM is the quality of having experience, knowledge and good judgment or being able to know the end from the beginning. Simply for perspective it would be like finding yourself on a road map and then picking a destination point. Looking at your map, you now can see your end from your beginning.

INSTRUCTION: This word will take different forms as we go along like *Knowledge, good doctrine, my word, etc.…* But what they all stand for in a nutshell is "FACTS." Information that is irrefutable.

UNDERSTANDING: I've seen this word bounce around and baffle people for some time. In the evangelical and the secular world alike. Everyone wants to understand how to do something, but it gets lost when they only want it to work their way. What was revealed to me was the simplest definitions for understanding; especially when it comes to our faith walk. It means "to accept the facts given."

Stay with me here because the pattern that we are discussing never changes. But at this point the wording starts to morph.

START—PRESENT—END—START

Is now:

WISDOM—KNOWLEDGE—WISDOM
UNDERSTANDING

Without the first outline of the pattern that was shown in John 1, I would never have been able to see it in Proverbs 4 to connect the word exchange. Like I said, your eyes must see the purity of what's being decreed to you (Proverbs 3:5-7). This, hopefully, has prepared you to see what very well is going to revolutionize your life. This pattern or tool is user-friendly. In other words, it is available for any age group, and the only product warning is for those who choose not to use it.

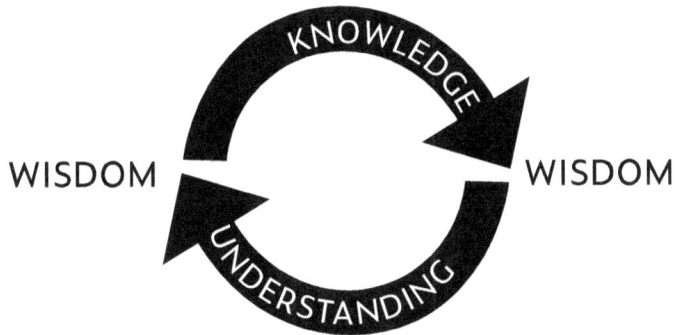

3

THE PRINCIPLE THING

PROVERBS 4:7-8 *Wisdom is the principle thing; therefore get wisdom: and with all thy getting get understanding. Exalt her, and she shall promote thee: She shall bring thee to honor, when thou dost embrace her.*

These verses are explaining the outline of the pattern and its benefits. It opens by telling us that **WISDOM** is our fundamental starting point and that no matter what else you are doing; you must get wisdom's foundation. Without wisdom being established first, foolishness and instability will run rampant in your life. Remembering what the definition of wisdom is (knowing the end from the beginning) reminds me of the old saying, "if you don't stand for something, you'll fall for anything." Think about if someone comes to your door wanting to sell you something or to force you to sign some petition. When the conversation begins at hello, you already know that this is not going to happen. And guess what? It doesn't. They are sent packing just as fast as they came. This only transpired because of your predetermined position regarding this specific scenario. Or maybe they stayed? But again, it was your choice. Unlike you, some people are pushed and victimized into situations like this simply because they don't know what their stance is in respect to these interactions. Then it costs them money, or even worse it steals their time. This is a picture of wisdom or a lack of. The first lesson of the pattern is to always seek to know your start and end.

In the next portion of verse seven, it mentions understanding after wisdom and nothing else. Until you look at the conjunctive phrase, "and with all thy getting." Outside of wisdom and understanding there is something else I'm supposed to be getting. What? The answer is "**KNOWLEDGE.**" Knowledge of what? Simply put: The facts. For example, Jesus is a Jewish Rabbi. Jesus was born in Galilee and was crucified. All of these are facts. It is vital to our faith walk to stockpile as many of these facts as possible. *Study to shew thyself approved unto God, a workman that needeth not to be ashamed, rightly dividing the word of truth.* 2 Timothy 2:15 The keyword here is "Study!"

STUDY—The devotion of time and attention to acquiring knowledge on a subject or situation.

This is a vital part of the pattern. Keep in mind as we study to gain all this factual knowledge that we do, so remembering that information is not the end-all. I've encountered many great bible experts that can quote mass quantities of scripture to the point it was like the bible was being read in their ear via Bluetooth. Awhile impressive, if it's not plugged into the pattern, there is no difference between that and having a car full of gas and no keys.

EXAMPLE OF TRUTH VS. FACT:

For believers and non-believers, we can agree that any verse in the bible says what it says, like John 3:16 *for God so loved the world that he gave his only begotten son.* We can agree because it's a fact like 2+2=4. Facts are not the disconnect. That only comes when we start discussing the second key in 2 Timothy 2:15, "TRUTH."

TRUTH—the real facts about something.

The state of truth is where we must find mastery of our position in knowledge. Look around you. Take note of what you see, how you feel, and what is on your mind. Because this is your reality based on your perception of environmental facts. My younger brother and I are very similar. Raised up in the same house with the same father and mother, we have uncanny moments that would seem as if we were reading each other's minds. However, on the other side of the coin, we process facts differently thus causing us to stand in two different realities of truth. Let's say both of us went to see a movie together. Yet when we come out from watching the same film, both of us carry two different realities of truth about what was seen.

A great visual example of facts vs. truth is to take five unopened cans of soda — three regular and one diet and one seltzer. At a glance, all of them seem to be the same (size, material, etc…). Now take a bucket of water and begin to place each can in the water. What happens? Three of the cans sink to the bottom, and two of the cans float at the top. Why? Aside from each can having a similar appearance, there was another group of factors that set them apart although unpresented to the naked eye. These unseen internal ingredients carried more influence on the can's behavior in the water than its outward characteristics could feature. All the facts shown by the cans observable surface were submitted to the cans innermost or core truths.

This goes on all the time between believers and non-believers. But even worse, it happens between fellow believers. The facts stand, but the reality of the truth seems skewed. 2 Timothy 3:7 *Ever learning, and never able to come to the knowledge of the truth.* In other words, as much as we've taken in and as strong in information as we have become, it's all useless without a reality to ground it on. What happens if you don't ground electricity? Harm will come to anyone close to the current and even death. Therefore, so many have been hurt and destroyed in the church. We have wielded the information or knowledge of the Word without grounding it in the truth of Jesus' reality.

So, how does this conflict happen? Look at salvation, the single most important event in Christianity. We take a new convert through some scriptures (ex. John 3:16/Romans 10:9-10), we have them repent of sin and confess Jesus as Lord. Everything is now well in the eyes of both parties. But if this individual walks away with just the information of what he/she has done, what happens when the knowledge is tested by their previous reality (B.C.)? Believers have walked this out so many times taking for granted that the newly born Christian will know what to do. And as a result, here is an ill-equipped believer that is stuck in salvation 101 because they were never taught how to ground life facts into Jesus' reality.

Peter shifted into Jesus' reality when he walked on water. As the Lord told him to come, his reality faded, and a new reality of truth became his when his foot hit the water. But then, almost immediately, the old reality regained its position when the new information was tested (Mathew 14:27-33). Now at this point is where I've seen so many get lost. They sink, and no one grabs them as Jesus grabs Peter. Not only did he grab him, but he also encouraged him using the moment to ask a teaching question: Mathew 14:31 ...*O thou of little faith, wherefore didst thou doubt?* Or in the way I would ask my kids, "Hey why are you worried? Don't you know daddy is right here?" Now look at verse 33: *Then they that were in the ship came and worshiped him, saying,* of a truth *thou art the Son of God.*

They now could see that Jesus walked in a completely different truth than they were in. We must accept the knowledge of Christ and the reality that he is the *truth* (John 14:6).

4

"KNOWING WHEN FACTS NEED A NEW TRUTH."

In Mark 5, there was a certain woman with an issue of blood. She had this problem for 12 years. The medical community of her time tried everything they knew to do according to the facts of their reality. She spent all her money with the belief that her issue would be cured. Instead, it only persisted. Until the moment came when she heard of Jesus. In an instance two truths came face to face. One reminding her of all the time and money spent in hopes of curing this issue; which only reinforced the hopelessness of her situation. The other came as she heard (Romans 10:17 ERV, So faith comes from hearing the Good News and people hear the Good News when someone tells them about Christ), what Jesus is capable of, then seeing the word made flesh right before her eyes was the catalyst, she needed to propel her out into her miracle. All the verities of her past were no longer the certainties of her future. Then when she touched the hem of Jesus' garment, not only was she cured. She was now living in a new actuality of truth, which nullified all doubts of her having a healthy and prosperous future.

ACTIVE UNDERSTANDING

Hopefully, you now have clarity on where you stand and where you're going to finish. Complimented with the knowledge of God's truth. All that is left to the pattern is the intermingling of the two, bringing about our active understanding. According to Wikipedia: Understanding is a psychological process related to an abstract or physical object, such as a person, situation, or message whereby one can think about it and use concepts to deal adequately with that object. For example, If I were to throw a tennis ball at a wall over and over, catching it as it bounced off the wall, and while doing this, I varied the speed of the throw as well as the height. Each time the tennis ball returned I would have to deal with its varied positions and speed to catch it. The more I performed the activity, the better my understanding becomes of the ball's reactive movements, causing me to be faster and more efficient at catching and throwing the tennis ball. The correlation between this example of understanding and the application of your faith is truly amazing. You want to go further; do you want to fly higher? This is where you want to be within the pattern. People often say they understand something and whether they indeed do or not can never be seen or proven because of their passive stance. Not unlike the tennis ball the pattern requires you to engage through active understanding. In Proverbs 4 after it says, "get understanding." Four words should be focused on as they are the keys to activating your understanding:

EXALT, PROMOTE, HONOR & EMBRACE

Each of these words carries distinctively different, yet harmonious meanings when observed through the Hebrew text. Not to bore you with all the details, let us look briefly at their meaning within the verse. Proverbs 4:8 says, Exalt her, and she shall promote thee: She shall bring thee to honor when thou dost embrace her.

EXALT—to lift up reflexively; without conscious thought; automatically.

I can recall a time when each of my kids were infants and how much effort would go into them, attempting to hold up their heads. Their mother, trying to get them to turn and respond to her voice; they would produce these hysterical herculean feats as they tried to figure out how to turn and get their heads in position to see what was going on. Fast forward to now as with any healthy child or adult, turning their heads in response to mama's call, doesn't even require thought unless they suffer from selective hearing loss, (which is an entirely different book). The moment you acquire the ability to get wisdom in any given area and to process the knowledge that comes with it, your sole responsibility is to apply apply apply; until it becomes a knee jerk reaction. Just saying, "oh I exalt your wisdom God!" Or "I thank you for your holy understanding Lord…" does not cut it. Then you leave it in that emotional moment and don't touch it again for a month. This is not genuinely exalting God; even if your bad habit of doing so makes you feel good about it. That type of lip service is false exaltation, which only hurts you. Doing so is just disguising passive understanding as if it is active understanding.

PROMOTE—to raise or rear (children), cause to grow up.

Keep in mind that we are God's children. This isn't an organization where you're trying to earn your way to the top floor and a corner executive office. Implementing the Pattern allows us to grow mentally, emotionally, and spiritually. As we hit a new mark of understanding, take notice of the process that took place. You'll see the genuine rearing of our loving Father. Patiently nurturing us as he guides and redirects us to new heights. Keep promoting the pattern until it grows up in your life.

HONOR—to be heavy, be weighty, be hard; to bear up under anything, to endure adversity.

It fascinates me to no end how complete God's word is when you take the time to look. When we skim over the word honor and think of medals and podiums, then the power of the text is completely lost. Picture one of your heroes or a great man/woman in history. What was it that separated them from the crowd? What about them solidifying a place in the vaults of your mind as you recalled their memory; when asked about greatness? It's not the accolades that so many covet after, just to hold a space on someone's mantle. No, it is that thing within a person that allows life to shape and mold itself into what we see. Think about a blacksmith forging metal. Working tirelessly beating and shaping it until they've arrived at a finished product. That product, whether weapon or tool, should be strong and durable if the job is done right. But, regardless of the strength of the ware, of the hammer or even the blacksmith. The one tool that withstood the beating and the heat as it supported the metal's transformation was the anvil. The anvil endures. The anvil is heavy. The anvil is hard. The anvil is singular in purpose. It must bring about good through durability. Therefore, it is that abiding characteristic of the anvil's permanence that announces, "no matter what you hit me with nor how hot it gets, I will still produce good in the end." This is the continuity the pattern will establish in anyone's life (not just the A-listers) when you acknowledge the long-lasting honor that is hers.

EMBRACE—an act of accepting or supporting something willingly or enthusiastically.

No one can force you to enact the pattern. Nor can you fake your way through it. Allowing yourself to be dependent on the Word of God, while finding security in the knowledge that you get to choose, places the effectiveness of the pattern in your hands. Part of my zeal in the faith lies in the power I've been given to choose. God never forced anything on me as he presented himself as an option, not stopping me from going one way or the other. Have you ever seen something like a flower or animal in the woods and then tried to point it out to someone? Yet no matter how hard you tried, they just couldn't see the little woodpecker fifty feet away hanging upside down on the fourth branch from the top of that pine tree. This is usually frustrating for both parties involved. But I do know, depending on how important it is to the viewers to see the bird. They will enthusiastically grab the challenge until the woodpecker is revealed. Operating in the pattern is no different. Choose to make it a part of your life as you are trusting and hoping with an unwavering heart. She will prove herself faithful every time. Just imagine mentally, spiritually and emotionally having more decisive reflexes, consistent growth, durability in every situation and an enthusiastic pursuit for more. This is who you are supposed to be and will be through your embracing of God's pattern.

[PROVERBS 4:8 EXALT HER, AND SHE SHALL PROMOTE THEE: SHE SHALL BRING THEE TO HONOR WHEN THOU DOST EMBRACE HER.]

5

GOD'S PATTERN VS. "YOUR PATTERN"

I think about the story of a pro golfer that was invited to play a round of golf with a very wealthy sheikh. After the round, the sheikh was most grateful, and as he thanked the golfer for his time, he asked if there were any way he could repay him? The young man replied, "oh I don't know. Just get me a club or something." Some months pass, and the pro golfer received a letter in the mail from the sheikh. Thinking back on their conversation, he thought to himself that this is too small to be a golf club. Then opening the letter his jaw dropped, because in the envelope was the title deed to a "GOLF CLUB."

As we walk around our world and talk to those that live in our society, we must realize the entire planet should be our focus, but our line of sight has been isolated to our street, neighborhood, city, or town. And those around us are living in the same limited visibility. Even if we are well-traveled, we become more aware of cultural differences but not to perception differences. Like the phrase, "it gets lost in translation" most accurately sums up the struggle of man when dealing with understanding anything outside of themselves. Look again at the golfer. This guy thought he understood what an appropriate gift was. He thought he knew what thankfulness, money, purpose of wealth, honor, sincerity, vision, etc. was; all of these played a part in the thought process of the sheikh, and though the golfer conducted himself properly according to the customs, his understanding of the question, "Is there any way I can repay you," most certainly got lost in translation. This happens all the time between individuals and groups as they interact with each other and with those from outside the circle. Most of the time, to their defense no one is intentionally trying to be disrespectful or challenging in any way. The problem lies in the fact that they all think they know and understand the other without regard for the more deep-seated ideology that's at work within the other. This is a never-ending cycle of confusion that gets more and more complex with the use of everything from the street someone grew up on to the origins of one's skin color. The sad truth is that these issues can never be fully understood nor resolved because it is looked at through man's pattern. This pattern relies on several key elements, none of which are reliable when the goal is clarity. Some of these factors are emotion, visual perspective, perception, memory, language, and attention. Now, with no way of knowing who is using which factors, or what combination of factors during a simple conversation, I think it's safe to assume that all of us can be suffering from cognitive distortions in one form or another. This means our minds are convincing us that something is real, but it isn't. It's almost crazy to imagine that our minds will rationalize inaccurate thoughts about an individual or group in order to harm itself. That's right! To harm itself, namely you. How is this possible? Just to put it simply, "we need each other." So, the more at odds we remain with each other; the more we are hurt. This all takes place at the beginning of man's pattern. It starts with uncertainty through a lack of attention, a bad memory or maybe a language barrier. I mean, we are supposed to yell and talk slow to someone that doesn't speak our language, "right?" Any competitive runner will tell you how vital it is to have a good start and in the application of The Pattern it is extremely vital to get out to a great start efficiently.

Jesus faced this same issue of trying to get people, usually his own to see the importance of a good start…

JOHN 1:1 (KJV)
1 In the beginning was the Word, and the Word was with God, and the Word was God.

Apostle Paul continued to carry on the mantle of God's Pattern and tried to show the value of knowing what our starting point is…

COLOSSIANS 1:17-18 (AMP)

17 And He Himself existed *and* is before all things, and in Him all things hold together. [His is the controlling, cohesive force of the universe.] **18** He is also the head [the life-source and leader] of the body, the[a]church; and He is the beginning, [b]the firstborn from the dead, so that He Himself will occupy the first place [He will stand supreme and be preeminent] in everything.

There was also back and forth with Jesus and the Jews on this very point that I believe is worth investigating. It's one of my favorite examples of how difficult it is for people to grasp what Jesus was trying to do in John 8:31-58. Within these verses, you will be able to see that the bottom line for anyone; husband, wife, pastor, bishop, brother, sister, aunt, cousin, friend, enemy, etc., is an answer to the question: Who is on the throne of your heart? And if you were to give an honest answer, where you stand in the pattern of your life will most likely make sense. Many people will state that Jesus is the Lord of their life and that he and he alone sits on the throne of their heart. It sounds good and even feels so good to say, but actions will always speak louder than words. As we acknowledge him almost simultaneously, we tend to rationalize our way into the power of the throne that we were supposed to relinquish. Just as we are now; there they stood in a conversation with Jesus debating over who has said so in our lives. Who is it that gets the start position? They would say Abraham and

God, but as you read through the verse you can clearly see that who was really standing in the starting blocks or seated on the throne of their heart was undeniably themselves. Upon further scrutiny of the verse. You'll witness a mounting frustration from our foreshadowing counterparts as Jesus continues to prove that he is the Starting point. Not you; not those men and women of faith we read about. NO. Only him.

WISDOM—KNOWLEDGE—WISDOM
UNDERSTANDING

6

THE CONFLICT IS CUSTOM FIT

As you continue to master the pattern and get a grasp on how to apply it to your life, always remember that the conflict is custom fit. You cannot hope to see the power of God in your life by mimicking other people or being frustrated at results that other people show when you feel as if you're doing the same or better. These can be ploys that the world and the enemy come at you with to keep you off balance and derail your progress. The conflict or the battle that you are facing is yours, and it has been specifically designed for your betterment. Just look at a few examples in the scripture. For instance, Moses helped to develop Joshua, who did not accomplish his journey doing things as Moses did. His conflict was custom made for him. David couldn't have had success like Solomon because the way Solomon had to operate was different than the way his father did things. And you can follow these examples all the way through the scripture. Now, it is no different than you and I. We can see other examples and allow them to build our faith knowing that what God did for them, he will also do and wants to do for us, but we must follow the pattern as it applies to our individual lives. Remember the setup of the pattern.

WISDOM—KNOWLEDGE—WISDOM UNDERSTANDING

Now, are you ready for another transition?

WISDOM—KNOWLEDGE—WISDOM UNDERSTANDING

Is now:
JESUS—YOU—JESUS

What just happened here? The pattern is starting to evolve, and at first glance it would appear it's just becoming more simplistic but as you look further where it trades a complicated appearance it gains power and momentum. Now the pattern starts to turn as a wheel, with completing one rotation after another. Whatever the issue, JESUS has been there. YOU have to go through it, but JESUS finished it. This is renewing our mind to the fact that what Jesus started through you, Jesus will finish. It is as simple as that! Look at your life and the different challenges or issues you have and are facing presently. Now, do so with the understanding that you are well equipped to deal with the situation. How do I know this? Because you are the one that's in it, I must face my giants' others have to face there's, but you are here to face this scenario head-on. And what I can tell you in dealing with the situation is that Jesus was their first, and he is standing on the other side expecting you to be there with him in Victory. The only part that seems to be unknown all revolves around you in the middle of your situation. But it was made for you. It has been custom fit for you not to assure your failure but really to guarantee your success. Think about the many great athletes throughout history. And there's always arguments in basketball about who would you want to take the last-second shot? Who would you want to be in that clutch situation? Many people will name a variety of athletes, but there was always one name consistently that comes up. I probably don't even have to say the name because you know who it is. Because when this individual was in his prime it seemed as if in the most high-pressure moments when others seem to fall short and fade away, he continued to Excel and go higher. Why is that? Simply put, he was made for those adversities. And it wasn't just the moment during the game that led up to those seemingly impossible game-winning shots. It was also the moments that he went through from the beginning of his life that compounded together to allow him to be who he was. We're not all made to take those kinds of shots, but we are met to shoot the proverbial ball in our own competitive fields. The Apostle Paul made references to running a race, and he talked about wrestlers and those in the arena. Making these kinds of comparisons helps us to understand the effort needed but also to emphasize that although there may be many other competitors YOU are Center Stage. Jesus has your back and your front, but you've got to stand up and allow the pattern of God's grace to fully engulf you.

7

CREATE YOUR TESTIMONY

Think about when you hear people referring to their testimony. Maybe you have referred to your testimony? It is always coming from The Stance of this is what happened to me and then how God kept you and brought you out of whatever it was that you' we're going through. And it always strikes me because it seems like most Christians talk about their testimony from a defensive position. The devil is punching me in my face, and God made sure that I didn't get knocked out, or God kept me on my feet long enough for him to win the battle. And this has come from generation after generation showing that this is the example of being a witness. Now don't get me wrong. I'm not saying everyone has taken this stance, and I'm not saying that God didn't keep you and help you through these situations. What I am saying is as we continue to mature in God's word and start to recognize the pattern that Jesus set for us; to make our own testimony. We should come to a place where our testimony doesn't just revolve around those hard times or fluke occurrences that we find ourselves in; it should start to be more about how my faith in God led me to take on different challenges because I know through him, I can't fail. I know the situation that I'm walking into right now doesn't look good. I know the odds aren't in my favor according to what everyone else sees. However, according to what I know and believe, I can call something that isn't into something that is.

Our testimony starts to be an account of Triumph instead of suffering and pain. The life of a Christian exemplifies the willingness to put yourself on the line for a greater purpose. Why do we do this? Because Jesus did it first! He did it for us and for the promise of a greater reward. Do you see the pattern here? Jesus—you—Jesus. Jesus made his triumphant entry into Jerusalem. Then soon after, he was betrayed and was on his way to the cross. Three days after the cross, he rose from the dead and set in motion the pattern that we must follow today. We make our entry as he did; living and doing the things that we know to do. Then there comes a moment of decision whether you are going to do what you want to do or what you must do. This portion of the pattern is what we call dying to self. It is in this place a lot of people get lost. A lot of people get weary, and many people fade back and start looking for opportunities for comfort. Just like any good plan, the pattern helps to keep you focused when your goal gets blurry. Have you ever heard those halftime interviews with a coach during a game when their team is down? Almost every time the statement is made that we must get back to our plan. The goal is obviously to win. And the plan that every team takes into the game is meant to direct them to a Victorious end. So, when things aren't going right for us believers, we must remember the plan or the pattern. Therefore, this portion of the pattern is focused on "YOU." At this moment, you must understand that you are always in the valley of decision. Deciding if you're going for the win and submitting to death just as Jesus did on the cross; being that he could have gotten down at any time. There was also a moment in The Garden of Gethsemane (John 18:4-6) when he stated who he was. And as the words "I am he," were declared from his mouth everyone fell to the ground. Jesus didn't lack power, and this means you don't lack power. But that power must be directed towards finishing the pattern. So, whatever it is that you must go through, you must submit willingly. God may have called you to be extremely successful in business. But as you consider what it's going to take to accomplish certain levels of business it becomes abundantly clear that this is not as easy as the get-rich-quick schemes would show. Nevertheless, this is the place that you must die to self. Sacrifice your sleep, sacrifice your comfort, or maybe even lose some money. However, if you recognize that this is the portion of the pattern that you're in it will be easier for you to stick to the plan. And hearing this some may say, but what's my guarantee?

To that my answer is the same guarantee that Jesus had that he would rise on the third day. Faith! Remember in John 17:21 where Jesus prayed, "that they may all be one, just as you, Father, are in me, and I in you, that they also may be in us... He prayed this prayer in faith, well before he hit the cross, believing wholeheartedly that he and God were one. The full truth of this was not realized to anyone else until he was raised from the dead. The rest of the prayer was in reference to us in the middle of the pattern. This is the only prayer that Jesus prayed that hadn't been fully realized yet. Because this is an ongoing fight for every Born-Again believer right now. We must believe and know that Jesus started this, and he's finishing this; if we stick to the pattern. Carrying our cross never; denying our cross and joyfully laying our lives down for others. Whatever it is you're called to be successful in, isn't always going to be easy. Christians are not supposed to be still. We were created to move. Even the best tailor-made suits can be a little uncomfortable; especially when they are worn with a purpose.

8

FINAL PATTERN

On this journey, maybe by now you have realized that each pattern is specific and applicable to your current level of Spiritual Development. One pattern or area of the pattern may seem easy to put into action. Then another area might seem a bit out of reach, and that's okay. The whole point and purpose of this book is to get you to start developing more in your faith walk. So, wherever you find yourself, that's exactly where you need to be.

Now in this final portion, we're talking about the final pattern transition. The last area we talked about was Jesus you Jesus, which was a great place for identifying Where You Are as far as pushing through hard choices and taking an active stance of faith through personal responsibility. This next transition as it has been shown to me is all-encompassing and very simplistic. But unless you have grabbed hold of and use the other patterns it can also be the most useless. We've heard it numerous times in prayers without realizing the true implications that are being stated. And so now we take a step from 'Jesus you Jesus' into the new pattern 'Father—Son—Holy Spirit.' This pattern holds all other patterns within itself.

The first initial pattern, **START-PRESENT-END-START**, is within the father. Think back to the verses referenced for the first pattern. (John 1:1-2) this verse is revealing to us God's permanent position in our lives. Nothing can come before him even if we try. He is still first. He is still going to be there in the middle and he is still going to be there at the end. When it's all said and done, he'll be there for the new start. 1 Corinthians 8:6 says, yet for us there is but one God, the father, from whom all things came and for whom we live; …and as we have begun to master these patterns by default we recognize when we say THE FATHER, it is not limiting him to one position but recognizing his omnipresence.

The second pattern, **WISDOM—KNOWLEDGE UNDERSTANDING—WISDOM** is within the SON. The second half of 1 Corinthians 8:6 says, … and there is but one Lord, Jesus Christ, through whom all things came and through whom we live. When we get to this pattern, we should have come to grips with the fact that everything we are, everything we know, everything we understand has come through the Life of Christ; the life in which we are living. So, when we state, "THE SON" it is our claim on everything that Jesus is. We should get as excited about this as sports fans do when they put on their team logos. Just imagine having the 24/7 faith-filled mindset every fan has during preseason. As far as most of them are concerned, their team is unbeatable, and they can conjure up those opinionated facts to back them up. There is no shaking these people. We should walk the same way with the only difference being; Jesus already won. So, our victory is based on fact in Jesus' name.

And finally, **JESUS—YOU—JESUS** is in the Holy Spirit. 2 Corinthians 3:17 Now the Lord is the Spirit, and where the Spirit of the Lord is, there is freedom. In all actuality, you are freer at this point than you have ever been. Which is exactly what you need for this next part... As stated before; The JESUS—YOU—JESUS pattern was primarily about YOU and your developing walk with Jesus. Now that you've become more comfortable with his presence, it will become more evident that the Holy Spirit has been the tangible substance of comfort all along. You and the spirit of the living God have become congenial partners. Notice the structure of John 14:26:

> *But the Comforter, which is the Holy Ghost, whom the Father will send in my name, he shall teach you all things, and bring all things to your remembrance, whatsoever I have said unto you.*

Can you see the **JESUS—YOU—JESUS** pattern repeated by the actions of the Holy Ghost?

- **MY NAME** = Jesus
- **TEACH YOU** = You
- **ALL** = Jesus
- **YOUR REMEMBRANCE** = You
- **I HAVE SAID** = Jesus
- **YOU** = You

It's so plain you'd miss it without the Holy Ghost. Have you ever looked at older couples and noticed that they start to look more alike with each passing year? In some cases, you would even think they could have been siblings. What has happened over time is the natural process of fusion. Through the time pressure and heat of a developing relationship, eventually two become one. And it is no different from your relationship with the Holy Spirit. The more time we spend with him, the more we talk like him, think like him and even move like him. Freedom, Comfort & confidence increase exponentially during this portion of the pattern. Because the Holy Spirit teaches you; who you really are in Christ Jesus. Galatians 2:20 *"nevertheless I live; yet not I, but Christ liveth in me:"* is the fulfilling of John 17:23 *I in them and you in me-so that they may be brought to complete unity.* So, when the revelation of this pattern within the Holy Spirit emerges, it will declare or proclaim that you're totally free and comfortable with who it is that You are in Christ. Because it's no longer the fallible person in charge that you once knew. The spirit of the Lord is now alive on the inside of you. And his spirit is the resolution within the final pattern; FATHER—SON—HOLY GHOST. Which has always been here; to deliver us the by-product of absolute freedom in this life. The first verse (Genesis 1:1) and the last verse (Revelation 22:21) of the bible clearly shows the Father, Son & Holy Ghost pattern. Proving through truth and fact; that the beginning usage of this pattern will drive you to the end for a new and more powerful beginning!

9

THE CHOICE

Here we are at a familiar moment. The point where the pattern renews itself and possibly you as well. There is always a point within a life transition where one can take what he/she has learned and start fresh. Or reject the new information and start over. No different than an Olympic sprinter coming to the same old starting line, but only this time; it's a year later with either tons of training, new experiences and maturity to pull from physically, mentally, and emotionally. Or approach the line with the assumption that last year's ability is enough for this year's start.

Now you've read this far in the book. Regardless of where you are in your faith walk and with the understanding that there are no coincidences. What will you do? As you read the last word, you'll have successfully arrived at an end. You are present now, in the place that the Holy Ghost is trying to speak to you from his portion of the pattern about your next start...

www.ingramcontent.com/pod-product-compliance
Lightning Source LLC
Chambersburg PA
CBHW071038080526
44587CB00015B/2675